06/08/06

To

Virgi...

Thank you for your
Support vota Rumba

VJ

A POETRY TRILOGY

Streets Paved with Gold
Return to the Caribbean
Children of the First Generation

The 'Empire Windrush' arriving
at Tilbury Docks, 22 June, 1948

VICTOR RICHARDS

authorHOUSE®

AuthorHouse™ UK Ltd.
500 Avebury Boulevard
Central Milton Keynes, MK9 2BE
www.authorhouse.co.uk
Phone: 08001974150

First published by AuthorHouse 4/14/2008

ISBN: 978-1-4343-7669-5 (sc)

Printed in the United States of America
Bloomington, Indiana

This book is printed on acid-free paper.

Contents

Children of the First Generation

Caribbean Quiz

Glossary

Foreword

I met Victor Richards when I was working as African Arts Producer at Nottingham Playhouse about 10 years ago. Next Stage Adult Education suggested that he should approach me about a performance he was creating. At that point he had not fully developed the play *Streets Paved with Gold*. Normally, as a producer, you don't agree to a performance without seeing it first. However, he was very committed and also very persuasive. This was not some stage-struck person but an artist who had a vision of what he wanted to do. I knew there was no choice – I had to put it on.

In fact, it was an act of faith more so on his part than mine to trust that his work would be produced in the way that he envisaged. It was a big success with a sell out audience.

This work has enormous educational value. Schools and colleges should make it compulsory text in their history or English classes; it is both for children who can trace their immediate families to the Caribbean and those who are from other heritages. As we are all aware, an important part of knowing *who* we are is knowing *where* we have come from.

Victor has achieved his success working outside the system. He has not jumped on to some particular trains. Nor has he waited for a producer to discover him. He has gone out and done it for himself. Even to the extent that he has managed to make it without the usual funding from the Arts Council England. That's pretty unheard of for an artist working in this genre.

I think Victor has recognised his enormous potential, and in doing so he is drawing out the potential in others through the medium of theatre – and in particular this play. He is uniting communities of people and empowering them as well as providing a role model for youngsters and connecting young and old. He is a contemporary griot, communicating through his work.

Above all, he is educating. As Nelson Mandela once said, education is the most powerful weapon which you can use to change the world. And in this subtle arts-led way, he is managing to do that. Not just in the UK, but internationally.

I would like to congratulate Victor Richards on publishing this poetry book adapted from his plays. I hope that this book will be read by many people – not just by the general public but also by the young generation. I look forward to the next chapter in his burgeoning career.

Principal Lecturer, Arts Management
De Montfort University
Tony Graves

Introduction

The brilliance of Victor Richards as actor, playwright and poet shines through in this poetry trilogy. As a playwright, Victor created the character Augustus Cleveland Johnson, an early immigrant who travelled from Barbados in 1948 on the *Empire Windrush* and landed on the shores of England. In the stageplay **Streets Paved With Gold**, Victor chronicles the experiences of Augustus Cleveland Johnson from the moment he landed, some sixty years ago, to the eve of his departure back to Barbados.

Over the past ten years, Victor has performed this successful one-man play on three continents. It was therefore a natural progression for him to pen and perform **Return to the Caribbean**, the second stageplay in his trilogy, in which the actor dramatizes the contrasting experience of Augustus, on his return to the Caribbean.

Children of the First Generation rounds off the trilogy. Victor's portrayal is convincing, as he portrays the character of Granville, the son of Augustus Cleveland Johnson. As a child born of the first generation of immigrants, Granville highlights the cultural and social change that has occurred with the passage of time in England. This trilogy has the potential of becoming an education tool for the now generation, and for generations to come.

Victor's trilogy has found itself in book form by virtue of his tireless interaction with young black pupils and students in the informative workshops that he conducts throughout the inner cities and provinces of England. In his after-performance question and answer sessions too, nostalgia rings loud with his older audiences.

This trilogy can be perceived as a permanent reminder of Victor Richards's creativity and powerful performance – long after the curtain goes down on his plays.

Author
Ainsley McKenzie

Acknowledgement

It has given me great pleasure creatively writing and performing my work over the years, not just for theatre, libraries, schools, but also places I have never thought possible, I have discovered many wonderful people during my journey, people who have helped me to develop and have shaped my vision with guidance, patience, wisdom, understanding, and by helping me to believe in myself through the difficult times. Getting good ideas is one thing, but for them to become part of society and a part of everyday life, thinking, and teaching in education, it takes years of hard work, determination, persistence, dedication and a lot of passion.

In 1994, my friend Juliet Bernard inspired me to attend the Nottinghamshire Next Stage Diploma course at the Sandfield Centre, where I studied drama. I met so many wonderful friends, talented students and tutors. It was one of the happiest times and most life-changing periods in my life. The Director of professional theatre and training, David Johnston, and his wife Ava Hunt (also an associate lecturer) remain friends today. Geoff Bullen, who was Course Director of productions and the Diploma course (now Associate Director of the Royal Academy of Dramatic Art in London), inspired my dreams in believing that I could do this historic one man play *Streets Paved with Gold* – not just well, but successfully.

I was sent from the Next Stage to meet Tony Graves who was then the African Arts Producer at the Nottingham Play House (now Principle Lecturer Arts Management De Montfort University). He gave me a break to perform my play – this was my first professional work. Tony has since become my close friend and mentor over the years, He gave me tremendous support when I performed at the Barbados High Commission's office in London in August 2007.

Tina Campbell, a librarian by profession, has been a close friend for many years, and was there to help me from my humble beginnings. On my journey through life I continue to meet different people and have learned to give as much as I receive. Many thanks go to Ainsley McKenzie and his partner Maureen for their support, encouraging me to write this book, and for helping me to realise my new goals and possibilities. Through them, I realised how our destiny is in our hands and how it's up to all of us to make the most of what we have as time is shorter than we think.

Finally, I would like to give thanks and blessing to my lovely wife Reiko, for all her support on our fascinating, exciting and challenging journey in life, as this book marks a new chapter in our lives.

I hope that people reading this book get as much pleasure and inspiration from doing so as from seeing the live performances. It is also my hope that they'll share this experience with others and help document their parents' history in their own creative ways – just as I have done – for the world to see.

Thank you all.
Victor Richards

Baobab tree

(Bicentenary of the abolition of the slave trade anniversary 2007)

I am a Baobab Tree;
some call me 'Monkey-bread tree'.
I am originally from Guinea in Africa,
but *I* am Barbadian.
I've been standing in the Queens Park
in Bridgetown, Barbados for over 250 years.

Yes, it's been a long time.
I've been watching a lot of dramas from here.
Suffering, pain, sorrow, change, joy and freedom…

Many Africans were brought on slave ships.
Men, women, and children, young and old.

They were all sold to sugar plantation owners.
A life of handcuffs, shackles, chain, whips,
as they were condemned to servitude.

They worked very hard from sunrise to sunset.
Field slaves, factory slaves, skilled slaves and house slaves;
some were used as sex slaves.

The climate of the island is great for planting sugarcane,
but it has a merciless sun…
Sweat, blood, tears were the order of the day.

The slaves had to eat the scraps that their slave masters did not want:
pig tails, pig ears, pig foot, yam, sweet potato, dasheen and coco.
Little did they know they were giving away the best part of the food.
Fools!

Music and dance healed their tiredness from a hard day's work
and the pain of living away from their home Africa.
Beautiful singing voices and powerful rhythms,
fused with the energetic dancing and beat of the drum …

From continent to continent, and generation to generation
African to Caribbean.
Black and white.
Rich and poor.
We must continue to fight for freedom.

I am a Baobab tree.
Some call me 'Monkey-bread tree'.
I'll probably be standing here another 250 years,
watching more dramas under these blue skies in the cool breeze.
From what I can see
there is hope that we can all live together
in peace and harmony.

Streets paved with gold

(In loving memory of my mother)

She said, 'Listen to the streets that were paved with gold.'
She said it was her story that had never been told;
she dreamed of the high and she touch the low.
It's given her a passion for time,
but in her life she felt her soul,
in the streets that were paved with gold.

The winters here, the faces there,
create a feeling of despair.
But she still hopes and cares that one day society can cope,
while on this soil she can taste the air of a mind that is breathing fear.

And with all the rage that she felt then,
there were closer ties never seen again;
with longer nights and with more friends with sweet music,
it was a time she thought would never end...

Amidst her fear she had her stones,
her friends that she would call 'her owns'.
With her cousins and family by her side within her home,
her soul was bursting with pride;
and with her two grandchildren – a boy and a girl,
she was always saved from what was going on.

Now times are changing and new faces appear.
She has seen them before but it was not here.
She could hear the new lives as the old disappeared,
and hope is tinged with a sigh.
Uncertainty looms as the path becomes clear,
now the streets of gold are fading...

She never thought this time would come,
when she would pass on and go back home.
Now she can touch the sea and feel the sun.

Good-bye to the streets that were paved with gold,
after all these years, she is going home.
She is going home, she is going home...

In Loving Memory of

Estine Eulese Walters

30 September 1930 - 17 November 2007

Streets Paved with Gold

'I thought England's streets were paved with gold'
– *Augustus*

I came to England in 1948

I arrived on a cold, grey and wet November morning.
We dropped anchor at Tilbury docks.
I was a young man of 21 years of age at the time.
I looked sharp in my suit and tie with my grips (suitcase) in hand,
waiting to disembark.
There were so many white faces looking at us.
Blonde hair, blue eyes, green eyes, redheads.

Stepping off the boat, I handed in my passport and smiled.
But he never cracked a smile back.
People's faces seemed so cold and unapproachable.
I heard that England's streets were paved with gold.
I always wondered why.
A letter in my pocket had instructions and an address.
Waterloo Station...

It was as if I had landed on another planet.
Old and large buildings were very interesting to look at.
I exchanged addresses with people whom I sailed over with.
We all said we would keep in touch.
A lot of us were going to different parts of England.
We were waiting for relatives and friends to come and claim us.
Rumour has it that a lot of us, including young children
who come over on the boat *Empire Windrush,*
never got claimed.

We boarded the train

I managed to get myself a good seat,
then the train started to move out.
It made a lovely sound.
I could even see the steam coming out.
Just then, the ticket collector came in and asked me for my ticket.
He was very polite. It must have taken me at least five minutes to find it.
I was so nervous.
I suppose I was in a strange place and getting used to a different system.
I settled down after he gone.
I looked through the window and tried to imagine back home.
But my sunny, carefree days had come to an end
on the cold, grey and wet November morning.
All I could see was rows of houses and large factories
with black smoke blowing and green countryside.
The train made a few stops along the way.
It was nice, until we arrived in London where I seen more rows of houses
and more large factories with black smoke coming out.

As I got off the train and walked towards the exit
I was expecting to be met by Johnny Grant, my second cousin.
I noticed there was a small group of people shouting,
'Go back home, go back home!'
I began to get nervous again.
But just then somebody tapped me on my shoulder.
I was just going to raise my fist and curse some bad word.
I turn around and look – it was Johnny.
He said, 'Relax man, it's only me,' laughing at me.
But I was so glad to see him.
He hurried me away to a waiting car, an old Zephyr.
We headed towards Brixton; man, driving through London was great
sightseeing.
Broad streets, tall buildings, people coming and going.
As a young man at that time it was very exciting.

Somewhere to live

Looking for rented accommodation was just as difficult as finding a job.
I had to walk from street to street looking.
It was hard walking in those shoes.
Especially when you read such signs saying,
'No Irish, No dogs, No blacks."
I remember one morning,
I put on three pairs of socks, three pairs of underpants, my long johns,
all of my jumpers, my overcoat and my trilby hat.
I visited ten rooms that morning.
One of them I remembered very well.
I had to climb five flights of stairs and when I reach the top,
there was no carpet, the window was cracked,
it was damp all over and the single bed was
stained with pukey marks and it smelled bad.
The owner said to me,
'It's my best room, take it or leave it…'

West Indians arriving at Southampton, 24 October 1952

In Brixton at that time

Most black people gathered together in their own homes,
or little rooms they rented.
That was where the idea of family worship
and shebeens all began.
There was nowhere for black people to go.
No nightclubs or pubs in those days,
so we had to create our own entertainment.
One day I asked the barman for a pint of beer.
He said he could not serve me.
I asked him, 'Why not?' Then there was laughter all around.
I said, 'I seen the sign outside, it said
"Public Bar", not "colour bar".'

The dance craze in the Fifties was the waltz,
the quickstep, the tango, and the ballroom jive.
I sailed over with singers, dancers, teachers,
boxers and actors too. I said to Johnny,
'What kind of work have they got here?'
Johnny replied,
'They have a lot of work here for bus conductors,
factory workers, domestic services, and hospital porters.'

The foreman

I never got on with him.
I always knew the day would come
when me and him would clash.
Well that day finally came!
There was a lot of tension in the air and
everybody had started to gather round by now.

Johnny's eyes were saying, 'Just walk away.
Think about your family; you really need this job.'
Maybe he was right, but I didn't care.
I was a man with my pride at stake,
and this man was breaking me inside.

He kept taunting me and called me more names.
I couldn't take anymore.
I just tump him down, right down to the ground.
Johnny tried to hold me back, but it was too late.
It was all over.
Everybody stood looking.
So did I.

Barbados

The island where I came from, the sun shines everyday.
The skies are always blue
and fresh fruits and fish were in abundance.
We were happy, but our land was poor.
So, to find wealth, we had to leave our homeland.

But we hoped to return a better people.
I was a tradesman, a skilled carpenter.
But I had to take a labouring job,
even though I had qualification.
My image of England was all changing.

All my dreams and hopes were all crumbling.
You see, as a young man growing,
you never think of relationships, do you?
You just try to enjoy yourself, especially when you're fit.
You never think of growing old.

Young Jamaican boy looks after his family's luggage at Waterloo
Station, in September 1954

I met my wife

One sunny day, when I was going to work back home in Barbados,
I went up to her and I said,
'I have been watching you for a while.
And I was wondering if you was a married woman.'
I was lucky.
She smiled!

Well feeling brave with myself, I said:
'You look like a very strong woman and
I was wondering if you would consider marry me.'
Then she started to laugh;
I noticed the gap in she teeth.

She laughed so hard!
Everybody in the street turned round to look.
I was so embarrassed!
But I stood my ground and I gave nothing away.
She seemed to laugh for eternity.
Then she finally shut she big mouth
and said in a lovely soft voice:
'Yes! But you have to come and meet my relatives first.'
We were happily married over 40 years.
She was a good woman; she was my wife.
She wash, cook, clean.
And gave me two beautiful children.
A boy and a girl.
We managed in cramped conditions.

The Church

I went to church.
I always find myself falling asleep,
and Mabel have to nudge me.
The Kids always find that funny.

I miss my kids, Granville and Samantha.
They're all grown up now.
I promised so many friends and relatives
that I would keep in touch.
But when you have work all the blasted time,
you forget about things like that.
Things are not the same as they used to be.
Years ago we were a small community,
and everybody used to stick together.
But not now.
Everybody is doing their own thing.

I loved my music

Nina Simone's 'My Baby Just Cares for Me'.
My wife and I used to love dancing to this record together.
It was her favourite.
I remember one day I came home from work,
Mabel was dancing in the kitchen, singing
'I Can't Get No Satisfaction.'
When I asked her why she singing that ridiculous song
she said she loved the thin batty man Mick Jagger
in his tight trousers.
Well the Lord works in mysterious ways.

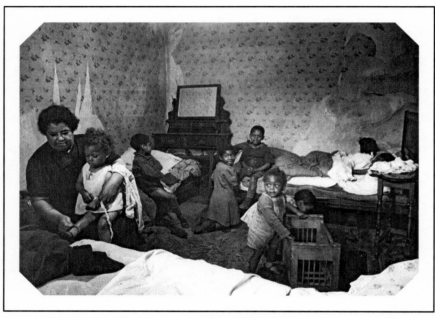

Crowded House - 1949: A large family living in cramped
accommodation in a poor area of London.

The Sixties

It was 1964.
Full of hope, we moved into our own home:
62 Belmont Close, Northampton.
The Sixties was a wonderful time, especially for the hippies.
Most English people started to free-up themselves.
Smoking drugs, free love, the flower power scene,
and the miniskirt.
Everybody was listening to
The Beatles, Cliff Richard, Marvin Gaye, Patsy Kline
and The Drifters…
In 1966, the England football team won the World Cup.
Mr. Bobby Moore was the captain.
We had some sad times too.
Martin Luther King, the civil rights leader,
was assassinated.
The Sixties was a wonderful time.
Life in England was becoming easier,
I could earn a little more money.
Employment was better,
I never really thought about going back home.
I always thought England was going to be my home.
You see, my five-year plan just didn't work out.

The Seventies

All the fashion seemed to be mismatched.
Young people never really had any style, in my opinion.
But I seen some hairstyles in my time.
Punks, skinheads, or cleanheads.
I think that's what they used to call them.
Greasers, mods and knotty heads.
And then there was the natural Afro.
But I never get caught up in all that stuff. Oh no!
I stick to my trilby hat, and short back and sides.
Nothing going to change that.

Racial Prejudice - 5 September 1958: An immigrant reading a sign on
a boarding house door which reads 'Rooms to Let -
No Coloured Men'.

The Eighties

Rock stars from all over the world united
to celebrate Nelson Mandela's seventieth birthday
by staging a concert at the Wembley Stadium.
The ANC Leader was released from prison in 1990.
When I was watching this on the television at the time,
I said to myself, 'Just look at that, this is history in the making.'

The Nineties, now we're in the Millennium

Another 10 years passed.
You can't even recognize England now.
Has it changed for the better or for the worse?
Black businesses are springing up all over the country.
Now we have black and Asian police, barristers
and even solicitors too.
It's wonderful to see, but we need more of them.
The Polish family from down the road now have the deli;
the Italians have the ice-cream businesses;
and the Chinese people their takeaways.
It's wonderful to see, but we need more of them.

My pension

Every Wednesday I go to collect my pension.
I meet an old friend of mine: his name is George.
We do the rounds you know.
We start at the community centre,
play a few games of darts and dominoes;
then we always move on to the Queen's Head
for a spot of lunch.

A pint of Guinness.
Then we always end up at the Conservative Club.
I sit there listening to these old white men
swapping old time jokes; and George, always talking
about the Second World War.
And just before I fall off to sleep,
they start to talk about the cricket.
Cricket!
Well, that's when I wake up and jump in the conversation.
You see, nobody can talk about cricket more than me.
I remember I had an opportunity to join the West Indian team,
but if it was not for the headmaster catching me with his daughter
I would have been well away.

1962: old grips (suitcases), old furniture

Looking back

Looking back over the last 50 years,
I can honestly say I have no regrets.
Life is a wonderful and precious thing.
You hold it in the palm of your hands,
water, feed and clothe them, and watch them grow.
Nobody can beat life, but we all lose it in the end.
I took early retirement.
I got a golden handshake and this gold watch.
In the Lord Mayor's chamber.
It was a grand occasion.
I was the first black housing manager in Northampton.

'We going home'

After all these years,
our children's children are still having to go
through the same racial abuse.
After all these years,
our children's children still have to suffer
the same racial abuse.
Well, I tell you! It's not right!
It's not right at all.
The Queen said: 'Welcome to the motherland.'
A mother is supposed to nurture her children;
Where was the nurturing?
When we came here, there was nothing,
only tents on Clapham Common.
After all these years.
We going home.
We going home.

Return to the Caribbean

Augustus feeding a chicken, back home in Barbados

The Caribbean

I've not too long come back from the beach
and had my shower, via de toilet.
You know, I have to shower two or three times a day.
It's so hot that within five minutes I'm sweating again.
I go to the beach most mornings at six o'clock.
A lot of people go to the beach before they go to work.
It's a nice feeling; I love the sea.
That's one thing I don't like about this place:
the flies follow you around everywhere.

My experiences

How did I ever get roped into doing this for the pastor?
I'm no speaker, you know,
but I've been coaxed into giving a little talk
about my life experiences in England,
and then as a returning national.
I could start by saying, 'England is a green and pleasant land.'
But I would be lying.
England, England.
'I arrived in London at Tilbury docks
on a cold grey and wet November morning.'
But that would take me all day and half the night, and it's another story.
What can I say without going through my whole life history?
'Ladies and gentleman; boys and girls,
thank you very much for inviting me to your church as a guest speaker.
I will try not to ramble on too much because
I'd probably put you all to sleep.'
You know, I used to drop off to sleep myself many years ago,
Five minutes into the sermon, I would be snoring away.
And you know how embarrassing that can be in a quiet place?
Mabel had to nudge me and the kids always found it funny.
Or I could do a preacher's thing:
'Listen here all you brothers and sisters; I was *Windrush*-bound in '48.
Travelled from paradise and hardship into England to find hope and
prosperity.
But all I found was coldness, and racial hatred.'
No, that sounds too harsh.

Going home

Once more across the sea I step.
But for the grace of God I go.
But this time the plane brought me back, not the ship.
Yes it's my first journey back in over 50 years.
Why is it everything about flying seems so final?
We assemble at the departure lounge.
They announce the final flight times and I'm there fumbling
for my travel documents and passport.
It leaves me feeling lonely and confused.
But when my flight lift off from Gatwick to Grantley Adams Airport in
Barbados,
it was just like a space ship taking off.
You know, six months ago I was a bundle of nerves.
Yes I was.
When I decided to come home,
I was having sleepless nights,
and going to the travel agent every two days to check for my ticket.
It was a big step but it was a nice feeling,
and you know once you book the ticket
there's no getting the money back.
Then you start telling everybody you meet, 'Me going home.'
Then there's the worry and talking to yourself,
thinking about what you need to take with you.
And, you know how we black people stay already;
we can't pack small no matter how we try.

The journey

I knew the time was right for me.
You see, I had a plan of action.
I swallowed hard, gritted my teeth, clutched hard
onto Mabel's picture in my locket and recited the Lord's Prayer
as I had my Bible in the other hand.
You would think I should be brimming with excitement,
but all I wanted was my feet firmly back on the ground.

The journey back home was about seven-and-a-half hours;
I slept through most of it,
except for when the stewardess woke me up for my meals
and when I heard the call of nature.
You know I couldn't eat a thing; I lost me appetite.
The food on the plane just didn't appeal to me at all.
All I wanted was my rice, peas and chicken with a piece of yam alongside it.

I remember as the plane was coming in to land,
I grabbed up my hand luggage.
And as we disembarked,
I heard the sounds of the steel band playing
sweet calypso music, welcoming me.
As I passed through the customs and showed my passport
my eyes were searching around.

Collecting my grips (suitcases)

The next thing was collecting my grips.
It took ages.
I tell you, I was panicking,
I thought they had left them at Gatwick Airport.
Before your suitcase arrive,
you would get these people in red caps and T-shirts
wheeling trolleys, approaching you time and time again and saying:
'Did you fly with British Airways, sir?'
When my grips finally arrived on the conveyor belt,
it was such a relief.
Then one of these red cap chaps came over to me.
'Your suitcases, sir?'
I tried telling him they are my grips, I can manage them myself,
but he just grab them saying, 'Don't worry man…',
and how he'll look after me if I look after him.
I wasn't exactly sure what he meant,
but I could see my ordeal was not over yet.
When I got outside I pushed my hand in me pocket,
I gave him one English pound coin, and thanked him.
But he just stood there with his hand firmly held out.
He looked in his hand then looked at me.
If looks could kill I would be dead already.
He only carried my luggage 100 yards.
In England that would be free.

A street market in Barbados

My son and daughter

Four times, I imagined Granville walking towards me,
and once Samantha.
But it couldn't be she.
From childhood, she always dreamed of America.
So, it was no surprise to me when she took off to Florida,
and her brother to Barbados – both doing well.
Then a sinking feeling filled the pit of my stomach.
What if I didn't recognise my own son or daughter?
Or them me?
I searched my pockets for the letter Granville wrote me.
I checked for the address and telephone number,
then went to make a phone call
and realised I did not have any Bajan change on me.
Then I hear, 'Dad, Dad, is that you?'
I turned around to look; it was a man's voice, clear and familiar.
It was my son Granville.
He was running towards me with a big smile on his face,
waving his arms in the air just like a child.
For a few brief moments we just gazed at each other.
You know when you can't find the words to express
yourself and your feelings just take over?

The heat

A sense of excitement came over me.
Beads of sweat came running down my face at the same time.
It was so hot.
I realised the suit I was wearing was totally inappropriate.
All I could see was black people everywhere, doing everything,
running everything – foreign exchange, enquiry desk and security.
Even some white people were talking Bajan too;
it was wonderful to see the changes.
People still go about their business without rushing around;
in that respect time had stood still.
Now there were shopping centres, offices, apartment blocks and luxury
hotels.
There was a strong sense of tourism about the place.
It was nothing like this when I was here.

Barbados - our rich heritage

The Sun shone so brightly on my face, it made me squint,
I thought I was going to pass out.
I remembered some of the places I went to as a boy:
Golden Beach, Archers Bay, Cherry Tree Hill, just to mention a few.
Just then, Granville pulled up in this big American car.
I could not believe it.
I said: 'You look like one of those big Hollywood stars son.'
He just smiled and loaded my grips into the boot of the car.
It was nice and comfortable; it kind of reminded me
of when my cousin Johnny picked me up from
Waterloo station in a brand new Zephyr.
Anyway, Granville started the car up, then put his foot down and we were
away.
As we drove along with the windows wound down,
the breeze on my face, together with the sweet Calypso music
playing on the radio, was the nicest feeling I ever had.
I was surprised how good the roads were.
I saw some brightly coloured houses
and fruit traders along the way.
It all seems to look so much more beautiful than I remembered.
Barbados – our rich heritage.

Reunited with family and friends

My daughter Samantha ran out followed by several others,
all cheering and shouting, 'Welcome home!'
I wasn't expecting that kind of fuss;
they must have invited everybody in the district.
I was overwhelmed; it was a grand occasion.
I could feel the tears welling up in my eyes;
I knew I couldn't hold them back any longer.
I got out of the car, Samantha ran towards me.
She's so beautiful.
I could not believe this was my baby girl, all grown up.
She looked just like her mother; I hugged her, and she was crying too.
I was the happiest man alive.
I held onto her hand and walked towards the rest of the guests.
I really didn't remember some of these old-timers,
but I made out that I did.
But the best part of my homecoming was
when I saw my grandchildren for the first time:
Justina and Nelson, all grown up, they were delightful.
How they reminded me so much of Granville and Samantha
when *they* were growing up.

Old friends

I arranged with Granville the next day for him to take me
to see a few old domino friends:
Obidiah Stewart, Roland Gordon, Barkie Johnson and Silvester Walker,
these four good men left England a few years back.
I spent the morning looking around my son's estate,
then in the afternoon my Granville went for a long smooth drive in his car,
chasing up my old domino friends, only to find out that
Obidiah and Silvester passed away and Roland had gone back to England.
And I didn't know that Barkie had gone missing without trace.
Old friends, you know how I came to know those four good men.

It was 1958.
I finished work one evening at eight o'clock.
I worked overtime; I should have headed home but I was thirsty, and
when you work in those factory places the dust gets on your chest
and I can't drink the milk like these white men – so
I decided to go for a proper drink in the pub.
In those days we black men weren't so welcome,
I walked in the pub and up to the bar of the Royal Oak;
I waited and then ordered a Guinness in a glass.
There were a few stares and coarse remarks, but
I never pay them any mind.
I bought my drink and found a little table in the corner out of the way.
I pulled out my newspaper and began to read the day's headlines.
A quiet drink, that's all I wanted.
Unknown to me then,
Roland, Silvester, Obidiah and Barkie entered.
I never saw them at first until somebody punched a tune on the jukebox.
As I sipped my drink, I caught sight of all four men
and nodded my head as a sign of acknowledgement.
Instead of reading, I found myself watching them more and more.
I rather got the impression they can't have been in England long.
It was the way they seemed to engage in conversation
with the attractive barmaid behind the counter;
Barkie offered her a drink and lit her cigarette with his.
The jukebox played one more record,
Roland leaned over and said something funny that made her laugh.
I found out later he'd asked her to dance.
That was a big mistake.

There were a few murmurs and moans; then came the bad language.
Someone kicked over the barstool and then a big fight break out.
Beer glasses started flying and bottles broke.

Then I realised these Teddy Boys had surrounded these guys,
at least 10 of them, some swinging bicycle chains.
I could have sat there, or quietly slipped away,
but I found myself slowly getting up off my seat...
Seconds later I was in the thick of things,
facing up to the ring leader (*they* called him Stan),
a real hard case, chewing gum.
He said: 'You're gonna get it mate.'
I never had time to feel afraid or scared as Stan came at me,
waving a broken bottle.
He lunged at me a few times, but
I managed to duck down and blocked his arm,
and made him drop the bottle.
We grappled for a while, and then I broke free.
Then a feeling of Muhammad Ali came over me,
and I seen my opportunity;
I gave him a left and right combination,
followed by the right upper cut that sent him crashing to the ground.
We really never had time to run
after the Landlord shouted,' I've called the police.'
When we turned to look around they were just coming in;
there were broken glasses everywhere,
it was amazing no one was hurt more seriously.
When the others saw what I had done to their mate Stan,
they picked him up and ran off in a hurry.
As for me and the four good men, we were locked up overnight;
the barmaid refused to help us with the police.
We were worried, but we laughed about it in the cell that night.
The next day we were cautioned and bound over to keep the peace.
I thought they would have deported us.
Silvester...
Obidiah...
How they cut off so quickly.
Neither of them suffered a day's illness in their lives.
Hard-working like myself, they also took early retirement too.
That was a day I will *never* forget.

A Jamaican family planning to emigrate to England, 2 August 1962

Carnival

Crop over in Barbados, it was a very special occasion.
There was no better time to come home;
the carnival lasts three days, but activities continue for ten.
People were jamming in the streets behind those big decorated floats,
with the music blurring out, and those lovely girls in their carnival costumes.
In the hot sun, the carnival ended up down the place called Spring Gardens.
My favourite calypsonian man is Mighty Gabby.

The speech

'Ladies and gentlemen, boys and girls...
Thank you very much for inviting me
to your church as a guest speaker.
I remember I saw a passage to England
on the *Empire Windrush* being advertised.
I worked hard, begged and borrowed money to raise
the twenty-eight pounds and ten shillings fare.
I didn't know at the time that I was one of
500 West Indians to make that journey.

'England was termed "our motherland",
but when I got there, there was no nurturing.
It was the first time in my life I became aware of
what racism really meant.
Nothing in my life could really have prepared me
for that journey – feeling completely
alone in a country that I realise I knew very little about.
The saying "once a man, twice a child" is very true,
but in my case it will be three times a child.
We didn't think that, fifty years on, we would make British history.'

You know, talking about history and ambition...
Before leaving England, I was privileged to witness
an open Celebration of Black Recognition and Achievements
for the first generation of the people who went there.
And I've been lucky a second time,
to see an award ceremony at the local community centre.
They were rewarding ordinary people
for achievements both big and small.
From the graduate to the child that has done well in a spelling test;
They even extending to the elder who has just learnt to read...

It make me feel good to see our youngsters on the road to success,
just like their predecessors before them.
I've seen some of the changes – some bad and some good.
England offered me the opportunity of a new life,
for my wife Mabel and children, which I worked hard to achieve.

But one thing it could never manage to offer me
was a true sense of belonging...
Here for the first time in years, I feel at one with myself.
I have my health, family and a strong cultural identity
that no one can take away from me.
I didn't believe I'd reach this Millennium, but here I am!
We may again be part of another historical moment.
Yes! This is my home – I've returned.
Returned back to the Caribbean.
Thank you!

Children of the
First Generation

Baby Victor with his father

The old family home

Mum cooking good solid food in the Kitchen,
Dad working at the factory, and
me and my little sister Samantha creating hell.
We were only allowed in the front room on Sunday,
family get-togethers or church socials that mum organised.
Mum put all the best furniture in this room;
thinking back, it was over-furnished, packed to bursting point.
There were ornaments in every crease and corner;
the walls were plastered with photos of relatives in England,
the West Indies, America and Canada.
It was difficult to decipher the pattern of the wallpaper.
We were frightened to move around in case something got broke.
We knew we'd get a beating.
The room was filled with brightly coloured plastic flowers.
Above the chimney breast was a framed portrait of Jesus;
most of my friends' parents had the same picture in their homes.
We had a Blue Spot gram – it was big and heavy, made from solid wood.
It had a sliding door that had a lovely drinks cabinet.
It could take the bass line.
In a corner was a large glass cabinet filled with china cups
on the top shelf and plates and crystal glasses below;
they were very rarely used.
The fancy chandeliers were something special;
every time I looked at them
I would drift off into my imaginary world.
We had the poshest house in the street…
Sometimes, when I came home from school,
I was greeted by the smell of fresh lavender or jasmine;
Mum was always cleaning…
But to smell fried chicken and dumplings was even better.
Dad regularly played dominoes with his friends on the kitchen table.
They slammed down the pieces so hard, or shouted so loud it gave me
earache.

My little black book

I found my little black book.
I called it my love directory.
You can do some stupid things when you're young.
It's full of girl's names.
I got engaged to Marion and Marva – then I found out later they were
twins.
Phyllis – she was nice and crisp.
Aloveen – was my dress queen.
Sandra – had a nice Coca-Cola bottle shape.
Patsy – Miss Sweet and Sexy, prim and proper,
she thought the way to a man's heart was through his belly;
she never stopped feeding me.
I'm trying to get her to do the catering for the party.
We are still friends; she is a nice woman.
But her mother, 'Miss Nosy' is too fussy.
Sybil – worries and problems, but she looked good
on my arm and she had charm.
Joyce – was nice, like rice, but every Sunday
she burnt the rice and it didn't taste nice.
Mum always said I have more girlfriends than clean shirts.
It's never been the same since she passed on.
I really miss her…
I could talk to her if she was here…
I'd be ok.

Victor, born on 29 May1959

My ambition

My ambition was to be an MC,
but my father had his views on that.
He used to say: 'No son of mine will have such a useless job.'
This is my lucky DJ hat,
I used to wear this hat morning, noon and night.

Now I'm the love doctor…
Coming at you live and direct on 103.4 FM in stereo
as we touch down with the number-one DJ.
We are going to bubble down nice and easy tonight as we go back in time.
As I dip into the coco basket and come down
with the musical selection to blow your mind.
Play it rude boy!
'This one is going out to the sexy body crew!'

I used to watch Mum, Dad and their friends dance in the front room.
Dad called it the church people's social.
One night I'd sneak downstairs and watch them through the keyhole;
I never expected the door to open.
When it did, I flew up the stairs faster than Jessie Owen,
but I tripped up and fell.
Dad caught me.
He said, 'Granville, why you not in bed?'
I rubbed my eyes and pretended I was thirsty.
I knew he would have given me a beating
if I didn't think of something to say quick.

Spinney Hill Park

One of the first things I did when we settled back here in England
was to pay a visit to one of my old haunts – Spinney Hill Park.
It holds a lot of fond memories for me.
Whenever my parents missed me from the house,
I'd be there with my mates:
Raymond, Howard, Dane and a gang of us.

We'd meet there most evenings after school.
We were all so competitive then.
Whites, blacks and Asians, we all played together;
we argued about who had the best bikes;
we squabbled about who scored the best goals;
we'd certainly joke about
who'd got to go out with the ugliest looking girls
at Spinney Hill Park.

It wasn't just a park.
It was the place to be, when we were young.
I remember there was a pavilion – it's no longer there.
It had a football machine and pinball games.
But best of all was the fast-food tuck shop, full of snacks.
I remember someone telling me
that the park used to be a race horse course over 150 years ago.
How things change…

Do you remember your first kiss and how wet it felt?
Isn't it funny how we remember the first anything we do!
How it stays with us all our lives.
I met my first girlfriend Irene, and had my first kiss,
at Spinney Hill Park.

Victor's school photo –
St Peter's Junior school in Leicester

My best friend Godfrey

Godfrey changed my life.
He was the reason for many of the problems we got into.
He had a different girlfriend every day.
At first I wanted to be like him, a free spirit.
But my father took exception.
From the first moment he clapped eyes on him,
he questioned him like it was the Spanish Inquisition!
'Who's your parents?'
'Which school do you go to?'
I wished I had never invited him home.
My Dad didn't like him, but I didn't care.
Godfrey had the same love of music as I did;
Godfrey was a cool guy.
But under the surface, he had his problems;
he was diagnosed as suffering from dyslexia.

The Church had a big influence on my life

Every Sunday.
My mother took me and my sister!
In our church, there was a preacher by the name of Archibald.
He took our Sunday school classes; his sermons would fill us with fear.
'Young soldiers of God,' he used to say, 'ungodly behaviour
will not be tolerated in this vestry.'
And then, the three N's would come in to play:
no sinful behaviour;
no fornication;
no rude boys or girls shall enter into the Kingdom of Heaven.
His words used to vibrate and echo down the hallway.

Victor is in the middle

Blues party

One night.
Sneaking out to the blues party with my mate Godfrey.
I would climb down the drainpipes like a cat burglar
after dark, and ended up at the Blues.
We looked mature for our age so we always got in.
They played cool soul and reggae until six in the morning.
Mr. Blues Sound System was the Man!
Seven days a week, God rest his soul.

The blues was hot! People were dancing close up.
The bass was pumping.
The atmosphere was electric; the air was musky with sweat.
Someone flicked their lighter to the music, and lit up their cigarette.
In that split second, I could see people dressed up looking so cool.
The women in their slick outfits;
the men in their silk socks and alligator shoes.
I just knew we were going to have a good time that night.
I always stayed near the exit, just in case there was a raid.
I liked to watch people dancing.

I scanned the room to see who was rubbing up with who.
Just then, I looked in the centre of the dance floor.
Who was there, smoking a spliff with a bottle in one hand,
whining so slow, with a big, big woman in the other hand?
None other than the godly preacher himself – Archibald!

I couldn't resist it;
I walked straight up to him,
and tapped him on the back of his shoulder.
He was ready to cuss me some bad word,
but he was suddenly stopped.
I said, 'Are you converting the sinners on the dance floor?
What happen Archibald? Your sermon is stuck?'
From that day onwards,
I saw the man of the cloth in a different light.
He couldn't preach to me anymore.
I never snitched on him.
It was our big secret.

Riots in the Seventies and early Eighties

Things were changing drastically.
The riots in the Seventies and early Eighties for one thing,
which led to bitterness and unrest,
for blacks, whites and Asians.
We, the black youths, were not classed as British citizens.
According to the media,
we were considered to be West Indians and nothing else.
(Unless we did well at sports.)

Protest for better policing, education,
employment and opportunities took place
in the form of street riots.
It was considered the only way
to be seen and heard at the time.
People began to acknowledge
the shortage of black representation across the board,
which needed to be addressed by government legislation.
We all knew that people's minds and attitude had to change.
Sooner or later.

My protest was subtle and silent in nature.
Not all of us have the guts to go out shouting on the street.
My parents would have been disheartened
if they thought I was involved in any physical violence.

Caribbean Quiz

Caribbean Quiz

The quizzes below were used in one of many activities at the ACES centre (African and Caribbean Elders Society) in Northampton, where I performed my plays a few times. The aim was to reconnect the elders with their past and stimulate their memories and minds. This is a good way of learning about Caribbean history for the younger generation (e.g. at schools) as well. See how well you can do.

Victor Richards

General Knowledge – Caribbean Islands

1. Ackee is Jamaica's national dish. By what name is it known in Barbados?

2. On which island was 'The Mighty Sparrow' born?

3. What is the national dish of Barbados?

4. What is the name of the island that Columbus first landed on?

5. Which island was Maurice Bishop prime minister of?

6. Which is the most easterly of all the Caribbean islands?

7. How many parishes are in Jamaica?

8. How many parishes are in Barbados?

9. What is the capital of Trinidad?

10. What is the capital of Dominica?

11. What is the capital of Guyana?

12. What is the capital of St Vincent?

13. What is the name of the volcano on St Vincent?

14. Where are the three peaks?
    a) Trinidad   b) St Lucia   c) Grenada

15. Where is the English Harbour?

1. In what year did the SS *Empire Windrush* arrive in England with the first 500 West Indians?

2. Which health minister invited West Indian nurses to England?

3. Who was the first black woman MP?

4. Name the other African/Caribbean MPs?

5. Where was Lord Pitt of Hampstead from?

6. Which African/Caribbean woman became a baroness in 1997?

7. Who is the chair of the UK's Equality and Human Rights Commission?

8. Who is Bill Morris?

9. Who was the most popular presenter of ITN's *News at Ten*?

10. Who is 'The Devils Advocate'?

11. Who was the first black royal press secretary?

12. What was Section 11 of the Local Government Act 1966?

13. When did the Race Relations Act come into effect?

Cricket

1. What were the surnames of 'the three Ws'?

2. Name two of the Test grounds in the West Indies?

3. Where is Bourda?

4. Where is Brian Lara from?

5. Which island is Phil Simmons from?

6. Which island was Larry Gomes from?

7. Which island was Easton McMorris from?

8. Which island was Eldine Baptiste from?

9. What was Viv Richards's highest score?

10. What was Brian Lara's highest first class score?

11. Who was batting with Brian Lara and made a century in the same innings?

12. Complete the following: George Headley, Ron Headley and...?

13. Which island is Bernard Julien from?

14. Which island was Keith Boyce from?

Food and Drink

1. Name four ingredients for a rum punch?

2. What is mauby?

3. Name four uses for the coconut tree?

4. Name four citrus fruits?

5. What is Tia Maria and where did it originate?

6. What is a roti?

7. How are cashew nuts grown?

8. What is the difference between a plantain and a banana?

9. The tamarind fruit is used in a popular drink ingredient. Which one?

10. Who brought the breadfuit to the Caribbean?

11. Green unripe mangoes are used to make which popular condiment?

12. In Barbados, what is another name for genip?

13. What are the main ingredients of Curacao liqueur?

14. What is a Daiquiri?

15. What famous Caribbean vegetable is related to spinach?

Caribbean Quiz - Answers

General Knowledge – Caribbean Islands

1. Genip
2. Grenada
3. Flying Fish & Cou Cou
4. San Salvador
5. Grenada
6. Barbados
7. 14
8. 11
9. Port of Spain
10. Roseau
11. Georgetown
12. Kingstown
13. La Soufriere
14. (a) Trinidad
15. Grenada

General Knowledge – United Kingdom

1. 1948
2. Enoch Powell
3. Diane Abbot
4. Paul Boetang, Bernie Grant
5. Grenada
6. Valerie Amos
7. Trevor Phillips
8. General Secretary of The Transport & General Workers Union
9. Trevor McDonald
10. Darcus Howe
11. Colleen Harris
12. A grant, given to employers to assist black and ethnic minorities from the New Commonwealth
13. 1976

Cricket

1. Weekes, Worrell & Walcott
2. Sabina Park & Kensington Oval
3. Guyana
4. Trinidad
5. Trinidad
6. Trinidad
7. Jamaica
8. Antigua
9. 291
10. 501 – not out
11. Keith Piper, who made 116 – not out
12. Dean Headley
13. Trinidad
14. Barbados

Food & Drink

1. Lime, syrup, orange and rum
2. A bitter drink made from the bark of small trees and boiled together with orange peel and various spices
3. Used as fruit, to make ornaments, to make huts, and the water makes a refreshing drink
4. Lime, orange, grapefruit, tangerine
5. A liqueur, made in Jamaica
6. A flat Indian pan bread made mainly of flour
7. On a tree that produces both a fruit and a nut. In fact, what is called the nut is actually the fruit which becomes edible after roasting
8. A plantain is bigger and longer than a banana
9. Angostura bitters
10. Captain Bligh
11. Chutney
12. Ackee
13. The main ingredient is the rind of bitter green Laraha oranges
14. A popular drink made from lime juice, sugar and rum. An American engineer invented it in 1896.
15. Kalaloo

Glossary

Glossary

ABC Islands

A term popular among the Caribbean yachting fraternity for three adjacent islands off the northwest coast of Venezuela: Aruba, Bonaire and Curacao. The first is a state in association with the Kingdom of the Netherlands, while the other two form the Leeward Islands group of the Netherlands Antilles.

Ackee

An evergreen tree, native to West Africa but now found in the West Indies, particularly in Jamaica. It was introduced there in 1778 when a botanist bought cuttings from the captain of a slave ship. The fruit splits open when ripe and the flesh surrounding the seeds is a vegetable. Some care is needed in its preparation as the Ackee is poisonous if not fully ripe or if not thoroughly cooked. Ackee and salt fish is a very popular Jamaican dish.

Allspice

An aromatic spice, sometimes called Jamaican pepper, obtained from the dried, unripe berries of the pimento tree.

Anansi (or Anancy)

The name of a spider who is the chief character in many West Indian folk tales. Although the name comes from West Africa the origin of the Anansi is obscure. In West African mythology he is connected with the creation of the world and prehistoric cataclysmic events, but in the West Indies he is a simpler being, reduced to playing the role of a cunning trickster.

Arawaks

A peaceable Amerindian people originating in that part of South America between the Orinoco and Amazon rivers. Having being driven from this region by more warlike tribes they gradually occupied all the Caribbean islands, reaching as far as Jamaica and the Bahamas by about AD1000. They were sedentary farmers and fishermen who lived in large groups; each group had a hereditary chief.

Bammy

The Jamaican name for a round, flat cake made from cassava flour which, after it has been soaked in milk and fried until brown, is used as an accompaniment to a soup or a stew.

Bay Rum

A sprit distilled from the leaves of the evergreen tree, Pimenta racemosa, which is related to the myrtle and native to the West Indies. It is used in the preparation of cosmetics and hair lotions.

Breadfruit

A native to the Pacific Islands, but now widely found in the Caribbean. The tree grows up to 60 feet tall and bears dark green leaves up to three or four feet in length. The fruit is round or ovoid, up to eight inches in diameter, and yellowish-green when ripe. The starchy fibrous pulp is used as a vegetable. The breadfruit tree was introduced to the West Indies in the late eighteenth century to provide food for slaves.

Calypso

A type of popular song originating in the West Indies, developed to its present form in Trinidad, and now widely recognised outside the region. It is played with variable rhythm, and the topical, often satirical and sometimes improvised, lyrics are sung rapidly without regard to the metre.

Caribs

An Amerindian people of the northern part of South America who, by the time of the European discovery of the Caribbean, had occupied all the Lesser Antilles. They were fierce warriors and cannibals, and the name Carib is derived from the Spanish word for cannibal. In the islands where they were strongest they put up a determined resistance to any European settlement. Great atrocities were committed against them in St Kitts and Grenada during the seventeenth century before these islands could be settled. Neither the British nor the French were able to gain control of Dominica, St Lucia or St Vincent until well into the eighteenth century. Their features are still to be seen today in the faces of many of the inhabitants of the Windward islands, but the only true remaining Caribs are to be found in the Carib Territory on the eastern side of Dominica. There, out of a population of around 1800 there are maybe 50 who can claim to be pureblooded Caribs.

Conkie (or Dukunoo)

A type of pudding made from grated sweet potato, coconut or pumpkin mixed into a stiff dough with corn flour, raisins, sugar, spices and milk. Having been divided into small quantities, and in order to be cooked properly, each portion is individually wrapped in a piece of banana leaf, tied up with a vein taken from the leaf, and steamed until firm. It is eaten hot or cold, usually as a desert, but often as an accompaniment to salt fish.

Daiquiri
A popular drink made from lime juice, sugar and rum, with each ingredient in a larger quantity than the one before, then shaken and strained through cracked ice. An American mining engineer invented it in 1896 when employed near the town of Daiquiri in eastern Cuba.

Evangelist
In the early Christian churches, the Evangelists were the writers of the gospels, the four books from which we learn about Christ's life. In the modern Church, evangelists are lay preachers. They are not ordained as pastors, but they assist the pastors by preaching at services.

Genip
A medium sized evergreen tree, native to the Caribbean. It has dense foliage with inconspicuous flowers, and produces round green fruit about one inch in diameter. When ripe, the thin, hard skin of the fruit is easily parted to expose sweet, cream-coloured, gelatinous flesh surrounding a large seed. When ripe, it is eaten raw and care has to be taken in preventing small children from choking on accidentally swallowed seeds. In Barbados it is known, misleadingly, as the Ackee.

Gig
A toy similar to a spinning top, used by children to play games.

Guantanamo Bay
A large sheltered bay on the South East Coast of Cuba, with an area of 30 square miles. It was leased to the USA as a naval base in 1903.

Kallaloo
A very nutritious dark green leafy vegetable related to spinach.

Maroons
The Maroons were slaves who had run away from the Spanish. The word maroon derived from the Spanish word Cimarron. Probably the best-known group is based in Accompong, Jamaica. Several hundred fought with the Spanish against the English during their successful invasion of Jamaica in 1655. At present there is also a community in Suriname called the Saramacca.

Mongoose

The Indian mongoose was introduced into the West Indies in the early nineteenth century to control rodents in the sugar cane fields. It was later considered a pest because of the damage it did to native animals and bird life.

Obeah

A form of sorcery or witchcraft originating in West African folklore, once widely believed in and practised throughout the West Indies. It is based on the belief that spirits may be employed to do harm to the living, that objects may be employed to do harm to the living, and that objects may be bewitched for the purpose of bringing misfortune to individuals. Specialists in its practice are called obeahmen or obeahwomen. Although long banned in most countries, such charlatans still exist, and a continuing belief in the power of the obeah is not confined entirely to the poor and the illiterate.

Pastor

An ordained minister of the Pentecostal Church. The pastor's role is to teach the congregation, pray with them, and care for them, often in a very practical way.

Pardner

The term pardner, which is used in Jamaica, has other names in other parts of the Caribbean like 'Box' or 'Sou Sou'. It is a way of saving money. A number of people would get together and make weekly payments. Each week, one person would receive the total sum. This way of saving called for a certain degree of confidence and trust in each other, but it was, and continues to be, routine among people from the Caribbean.

Port Royal

Port Royal in Jamaica is now an historic site and was once described as 'the richest and wickedest city in the world' during its occupation by the buccaneers who brought a great deal of wealth to the city. In June 1692 an earthquake destroyed most of Port Royal. The Palisadoes peninsula that it was built on was of strategic importance to the British who made it their naval base in the Caribbean during the eighteenth and nineteenth centuries.

Rastafarian Movement
The prophetic cult movement, which originated from Jamaica in the 1930s. Followers of the movement believe in the divinity of Haile Salassie, the former emperor of Ethiopia.

Rum
A colourless spirit, distilled from the products of sugar cane, mainly the thick brown syrup called molasses, which originated in the West Indies.

Run Dung
Food cooked in coconut milk obtained after grating the dry coconut meat and squeezing it in water.

Souse
A favourite West Indian dish made from pork, using the pig's head, tongue, and trotter. It is then soaked in salt water and lime juice before pepper, onion, cucumber and stock are added. It is served hot or cold.

Steel Band
A group of musicians who play instruments made from steel drums, producing a distinctive sound known as 'pan'.

Ugli
A hybrid citrus fruit, a cross between a grapefruit and a tangerine, developed in Trout Hall, Jamaica.